**HOW CAN WE
SAVE OUR
WORLD?**

sustainable

TOURISM

Andrew Solway

W

FRANKLIN WATTS
LONDON•SYDNEY

First published in 2009 by Franklin Watts

Copyright © 2009 Arcturus Publishing Limited

Franklin Watts
338 Euston Road
London NW1 3BH

Franklin Watts Australia
Level 17/207 Kent Street
Sydney, NSW 2000

Produced by Arcturus Publishing Limited
26/27 Bickels Yard
151-153 Bermondsey Street
London SE1 3HA

The right of Andrew Solway to be identified as the author of this work has been asserted by him in accordance with the Copyright, Designs and Patents Act 1988.

Series concept: Alex Woolf
Editor and picture researcher: Patience Coster
Designer: Phipps Design

A CIP catalogue record for this book is available from the British Library.

Dewey Decimal Classification Number: 338.4′ 791

ISBN 978 0 7496 8216 3

Printed in China

Franklin Watts is a division of Hachette Children's Books, an Hachette UK company.
www.hachette.co.uk

Picture Credits
Corbis: 10 (Geoffrey Clements), 13 (Hulton-Deutsch Collection), 15 (Jonathan Blair), 17 (Paul Souders), 19 (Georgina Bowater), 20 (Piyal Adhikary/epa), 21 (Peter Andrews/Reuters), 22 (Paul Souders), 24 (Christian Guy), 28 (Patrick Frilet/Hemis), 31 (Staffan Widstrand), 35 (Jason Lee/Reuters), 38 (Richard Klune), 39 (Wolfgang Kaehler), 41 (Qi Heng/Xinhua Press), 42 (Rick D'Elia); EASI-Images: 26 (Rob Bowden), 27 (Clive Sanders), 32 (Rob Bowden), 40 (Rob Bowden); Grecotel S.A.: 37; Mary Evans Picture Library: 9 (Grosvenor Prints); Shutterstock: cover (Maksym Gorpenyuk), 6 (Christophe Testi), 7 (Keith Levit), 11 (David Hughes), 12 (Jon Naustdalslid), 14 (Graham Tomlin), 16 (eAlisa), 25 (rebvt), 29 (Kitch Bain), 30 (Mayskyphoto), 33 (David Mckee), 34 (Tan Wei Ming), 43 (Mayskyphoto); TopFoto: 8 (Alinari); Whitepod: 36.

The artwork on page 12 is by Phipps Design.

CONTENTS

Tourism and the Climate Crisis

Tourism is one of the world's biggest industries. One person in twelve works in tourism, either directly or indirectly, and the industry earns US $6.5 trillion ($6,500 billion) every year. However, there are drawbacks as well as benefits to tourism.

The island of Maui in Hawaii is a tourist paradise. Long sandy beaches are fringed with palm trees. The weather is warm all year, and the Pacific Ocean sparkles blue in the sunshine. You can swim, go snorkelling, surf, paddle a canoe, or just laze in the sun.

For the islanders, tourism is a mixed blessing. It has brought in a great deal of money, but it has also created problems. Maui is only 77 km long and 40 km wide, but over two million people come to the island each year. The beach fronts are packed with new houses and hotels to accommodate all these visitors. The roads are regularly jammed with traffic, and the tourists' demands on the island's water supply have stretched it to its limit. Providing enough food for the visitors and getting rid of all the waste they produce places a huge strain on the island's resources.

The island of Maui is full of beautiful beaches like this one. However, the attraction of many of them has been spoiled by large numbers of hotels and other buildings right next to the beach.

Benefits and drawbacks

Tourism is especially important for developing countries, where the money and jobs that it brings are of great benefit. But tourists also produce waste, use up precious resources such as water and food, and cause damage to the environment. Recently people have become more aware of the impact that tourism can have on a place. Most tourists want to avoid damaging the environment. They would like to go on holidays that bring benefits to an area without also causing problems.

So how can we ensure that tourism benefits, rather than destroys, the environment? We have to take a new approach to the idea of tourism and think of ways in which it can be made more sustainable.

The roads in Maui were not built to deal with the two million visitors who come to the island each year. As a result there are many traffic problems.

PERSPECTIVE

Responsible tourism

'When we travel, we make positive impacts on destinations and communities, and negative impacts. What responsible tourism is about, is travel that does more of the positive and less of the harm.'

Justin Francis, managing director of responsibletravel.com

CHAPTER 1

Early Tourists

People have always travelled. They travel for their job, or for their health, or as pilgrims or explorers. However, this type of travel is different from tourism, when people take a holiday for pleasure.

Probably the first tourists were wealthy Romans. Many of them left Rome in the summer, when it became hot and smelly, and travelled to their 'second homes'
– villas or estates on the coast or in the countryside. The richest travellers had small villas, complete with servants or slaves, where they could stay on route to their summer home. Less well-off Romans stayed at inns (*tabernae*). Some Romans went on grand tours that took several years. They travelled as far afield as Turkey and Egypt to visit pleasure spots and sacred sites.

The Grand Tour

After Roman times, few people travelled for pleasure until the seventeenth and eighteenth centuries. During this period, the Grand Tour became popular once again. Young men whose parents could afford it were sent on a trip that could last anything from a few months to eight years. The tour was supposed to be educational, and the young men usually travelled with a

These ruins are the remains of what was once a rich Roman's summer villa on the coast of Tuscany, northern Italy.

tutor or guardian. Its main focus was Italy, where the men visited ancient Roman ruins, art galleries, palaces and other buildings. Often a grand tourist would have his portrait painted by a famous artist, as a reminder of his trip. He might also bring back souvenirs, such as ancient vases and statues. In 1733, the Duke of Beaufort brought back a marble sarcophagus (coffin) as a souvenir!

This painting shows eighteenth-century tourists, probably on a Grand Tour, and two artists at the Temple of Diana in Nîmes, France.

PERSPECTIVE

A grand view

'After sailing four miles from Ross, we came to Goodrich-castle; where a grand view presented itself. . . . A reach of the river, forming a noble bay, is spread before the eye. The bank, on the right, is steep, and covered with wood; beyond which a bold promontory shoots out, crowned with a castle, rising among trees. This view, which is one of the grandest on the river, I should not scruple to call correctly picturesque; which is seldom the character of a purely natural scene.'

In 1782, the beginnings of British tourism were marked by the publication of a guidebook entitled *Observations on the River Wye*.

The call of the wild

In the later eighteenth century, tourism for people with rather less money than the grand tourists began in Britain. People travelled to see natural 'curiosities' such as the Peak Cavern in Derbyshire and the Wye Valley on the border between England and Wales.

In the nineteenth century, large numbers of ordinary people in both Europe and the United States began to take trips to interesting places for pleasure and curiosity. The new railways that were being built everywhere made travelling much cheaper and faster. In Britain, people travelled to seaside resorts such as Brighton, Bournemouth and Blackpool. At first the visitors were better-off people such as doctors, lawyers and businessmen. But by the later nineteenth century, working people were taking short trips to the seaside.

In the United States, intrepid tourists made long trips to places such as Yellowstone and the Yosemite Valley. At the time, these places were very wild and remote. One of the most popular wild attractions was Niagara Falls, on the border between the United States and Canada.

FACE THE **FACTS**

The number of people visiting wilderness attractions in the United States has grown enormously. For example, in the early 1870s Yellowstone had about 500 visitors each year. By 1900 there were nearly 9,000. Today around three million people visit Yellowstone annually. Such huge numbers are bound to have an environmental impact on the area.

The artist Thomas Moran was one of the first white people to travel to Yellowstone. He went in 1871 with the US Geological Survey. The dramatic landscapes Moran painted inspired others to visit Yellowstone to see its wonders.

PERSPECTIVE

A journey to the Old World

'We are getting foreignized rapidly and with facility. We are getting reconciled to halls and bedchambers with unhomelike stone floors and no carpets. . . . We are getting used to tidy, noiseless waiters, who glide hither and thither, and hover about your back and your elbows like butterflies, quick to comprehend orders, quick to fill them. . . . We are getting used to driving right into the central court of the hotel, in the midst of a fragrant circle of vines and flowers, and in the midst also of parties of gentlemen sitting quietly reading the paper and smoking.'

American writer and traveller Mark Twain describes his trip east to Europe in *Innocents Abroad*, 1869.

The view down Monsal Dale in Derbyshire, UK. A railway line built in the 1860s brought early tourists to see Derbyshire attractions such as Monsal Dale and the Peak Cavern at Castleton.

In the late nineteenth century, the Scottish-American naturalist and geologist John Muir lived and worked in Yosemite. The area was being opened up for sheep and cattle grazing, but Muir argued that it needed to be preserved unspoiled for future generations. Tourism had made people aware of the beauty of Yosemite, and this helped Muir to win his argument. In 1905 Yosemite became the world's first national park.

Mass tourism

During the twentieth century, the numbers of tourists grew enormously. For the first part of the century, most tourists holidayed in their own or a nearby

The Great Wall of China was recently voted one of the seven modern wonders of the world. Over a million tourists visit each year. The most popular parts of the wall have been badly damaged by the large numbers of visitors.

FACE THE **FACTS**

The graph below shows the growth in tourist numbers since the 1950s.

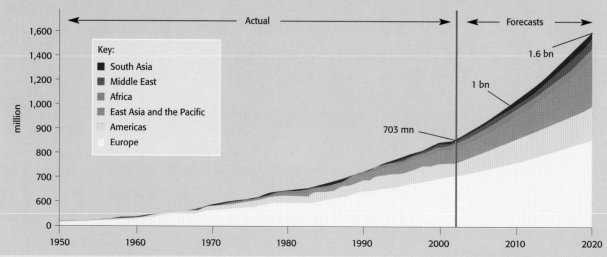

Key:
- South Asia
- Middle East
- Africa
- East Asia and the Pacific
- Americas
- Europe

Actual — Forecasts

1.6 bn
1 bn
703 mn

Source: United Nations World Tourist Organization

country. However, after World War II, turboprop and jet engines made planes faster and more reliable.

Jet aircraft revolutionized long-distance holiday travel. In 1939, it took six days to cross the Atlantic on a fast passenger ship. By 1959, with the introduction of the first jet airliners, the time had been cut to six hours. The faster journey made long-distance trips far more possible for people with a limited amount of holiday time.

By the end of the twentieth century it had become very cheap to travel by plane. Many people could afford to fly halfway round the world for a holiday. Places such as southern Africa, India, Southeast Asia, South America and the Caribbean became popular tourist destinations. As large numbers of visitors arrived in these new destinations they brought money and work, but they also made a heavy 'footprint' on the environment.

Passengers for Johannesburg, South Africa, board the world's first commercial jet airliner (a de Havilland Comet) in London, 1952.

SUSTAINABLE
DEVELOPMENTS

The turbofan jet

A major problem with jet aircraft is that they burn huge quantities of fossil fuels. This produces high levels of carbon dioxide emissions. However, the development of a type of jet called a 'turbofan' has greatly reduced the amount of fuel that airliners use.

A normal aircraft engine burns air and fuel in a combustion chamber to produce a high-speed jet of hot gases. However, this type of engine is only really efficient at supersonic speeds. In a turbofan engine, some air goes through the combustion chamber, but a fan at the front of the engine also pushes large amounts of air around the combustion chamber and out of the back of the engine. This extra air makes the engine much more efficient at cruising speed.

CHAPTER 2

How Tourism Affects the Environment

The number of people travelling abroad on holiday grows every year. When a lot of tourists arrive in a place, they have an effect on the environment. The buildings, the food, the water, and even the way in which people reach their destination may cause damage both to the local area and to the global environment.

We cause damage to the environment simply by travelling to a tourist destination. Cars, buses, trains, aircraft and most boats all depend on engines to power them along. These engines produce carbon dioxide and other polluting gases. Carbon dioxide is one of a number of greenhouse gases which help to trap heat in the Earth's atmosphere. It contributes to climate change – the gradual warming of the Earth brought about, in part, by human activities such as industry and deforestation.

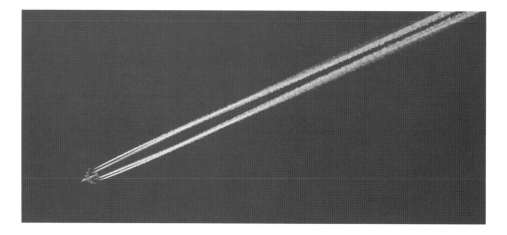

Today, airline travel is cheap in money terms, but expensive for the environment. A study by WWF found that 70 per cent of the carbon emissions from a holiday in the Mediterranean were caused by the flights there and back.

Acid rain

Vehicle engines produce other gases that cause acid rain, another form of pollution. Acid rain is water vapour that contains acid-forming chemicals released into the atmosphere through the burning of fossil fuels. It can cause damage to trees and other plants, and may also affect wildlife in the water, especially in lakes. Smog is a kind of fog caused by air pollution. It can cause breathing disorders and other health problems in some people.

Tourist travel by air is particularly bad for the environment. This is because, even with more efficient engines, jet airliners produce more carbon dioxide per passenger than any other kind of transport. Aircraft release carbon dioxide and other gases high in the atmosphere. These gases have a more damaging effect on the environment at this level than they would do on the ground.

The exhaust fumes from car engines can travel long distances. This forest in the Czech Republic was damaged by acid rain caused by traffic fumes hundreds of miles away.

FACE THE **FACTS**

In 2007, 903 million people travelled abroad for their holidays. By 2020, the number of overseas tourists is expected to reach 1,600 million (1.6 billion). In 2007, the most popular tourist destinations were France, Spain and the United States. However, an increasing number of people are choosing to go to less developed countries for their holidays. Malaysia and Thailand are among the top twenty tourist destinations. Bangkok in Thailand is the second-biggest tourist city in the world after London.

Somewhere to stay

Once tourists arrive at their destination, they need somewhere to stay. This is not a problem when tourists travel to large towns and cities where there are many hotels and apartments. But tourists often want to holiday by the sea or visit areas of 'unspoiled' countryside. There is often not enough tourist accommodation in these more rural locations. This means that hotels and apartments have to be built specifically to cater for tourists. New airports and seaports may also need to be built and roads enlarged to cope with the increased volume of traffic.

All this construction work can have a huge impact on the environment. Land needs to be cleared for new buildings. This may mean cutting down forests or draining wetlands. Forests and wetlands are important habitats for many kinds of wildlife. Wetlands also act as a kind of 'sponge' that soaks up large amounts of water when there are storms and rough seas. The draining of wetlands along the coast leaves the area at greater risk of flooding.

Dredging for sand or aggregate (gravel) greatly increases beach erosion.

Beach erosion

Clearing land can also cause erosion. Palm trees growing along tropical beaches are important for stabilizing the sandy soil. Their roots help keep the soil in place, and the trees themselves act as a natural barrier to the sea. If they are cut down, the beach may erode (wear away) more quickly.

When people obtain materials from beaches, such as sand for new buildings, this can also damage the local environment. Trees may be cut down for timber, and sand taken to make concrete. Even more worrying is the mining of coral reefs. These reefs provide beaches with natural protection from action by waves. In Sri Lanka, over 10,000 tonnes of coral are removed from the reefs each year and used to make cement for building.

A submarine takes tourists to see the wonders of the coral reefs around the Cayman Islands in the Caribbean. Submarine trips have the advantage that passengers cannot take souvenirs of coral from the reef.

FACE THE **FACTS**

Coral reefs are the most bio-diverse of ocean eco-systems. They cover less than 0.1 per cent of the oceans yet they are home to over a million marine species, including over a quarter of the world's different types of fish. However, 70 per cent of the world's coral reefs have been damaged by human activities, and around 20 per cent of these damaged reefs have been destroyed completely.

Using up resources

Tourists who travel abroad are mostly from more developed countries. When they visit developing countries, most tourists stay in hotels, where they expect efficient service and good food. They expect there to be bathrooms with a bath, a shower and toilet facilities. Hotels often have swimming pools, especially in hot countries; they may even have a golf course. All these facilities use up resources that are in short supply.

Providing enough suitable food for tourists can be a problem in less developed countries. A lot of the food may not be available locally so will need to be imported. Tourists are usually willing to pay more for food than local people can afford. As a result, food prices may rise. Local people may be forced to eat less, or eat poorer food because of such price rises.

Precious water

Hotel bathrooms and swimming pools need a regular supply of water. In less developed countries, hotels use far more water than local people do. Tourists also use large amounts of water. Studies have shown that they often use more water on holiday than they do at home – up to 440 litres per person every day.

Many tourist destinations are in warm, sunny places, where water is in short supply. If the available water is used for swimming pools and golf courses, this may leave little water for farmers to use on their crops. The Hawaiian island of Maui receives a large amount of rainfall. Some parts of the island have 760 cm of rainfall each year. But at the height of the tourist season Maui uses more than 65 million litres of water every day. As a result, recently there have been droughts in Maui almost every year.

Opposite: Jumeirah Beach in Dubai is a luxury resort for the rich. However, the area was developed so fast that it was being used by tourists before a proper sewerage system could be built. In 2009 stretches of beach were closed because of raw sewage in the water.

FACE THE **FACTS**

- **An average golf course in a tropical country such as Thailand uses as much water as 60,000 local villagers. It also takes 1,500 kg of chemical fertilizers, pesticides and herbicides each year to keep the course green and weed free.**
- **It is estimated that one tourist development being planned in Mexico will use nearly two million litres of water each day.**
- **A luxury hotel in Goa, India, uses as much water as five villages, and each hotel guest uses 26 times the amount of electricity that a local person uses.**

Waste and contamination

Tourists don't just use up resources, they also produce large amounts of solid waste and sewage. The solid waste is deposited in local landfill sites, while the sewage is frequently pumped into rivers or the sea. In less developed countries, the sewage is often untreated. It therefore contains large numbers of microbes which can cause diseases in humans or other animals that drink the water. Sewage can sometimes overload the water with nutrients, resulting in the growth of large numbers of microscopic algae. The algae use up all the oxygen in the water, which means that other water life cannot survive.

With large numbers of tourists visiting beaches, litter becomes a major pollution problem. This beach in Andhra Pradesh, India, is littered with plastic waste.

Tourist activities

People go on holiday to enjoy themselves. Tourists visit the seaside to swim, sunbathe, and perhaps go scuba diving or sailing. They travel to the mountains to ski, walk or climb. Some people go on holiday to see ancient buildings, churches, museums and other attractions. Some travel to national parks and nature reserves to watch wildlife in its natural habitat. All these activities can cause damage to the environment and to local communities.

More about reefs

Some parts of the world, such as Australia, Thailand, Sri Lanka and the Caribbean, are renowned for their beautiful coral reefs. However, unless tourism is carefully controlled, visitors can end up destroying the coral reefs they come to see. Sometimes tourists take small amounts of coral from the reefs, or buy souvenirs made from coral. This may not seem as bad as mining tonnes of coral from the reefs (see page 16), but if thousands of tourists take or buy coral every year, it can do almost as much damage to the reefs as coral mining.

Rainforest treks

At Volcano National Park in Rwanda, Africa, tourists can see some of the world's small remaining population of Highland gorillas. People can trek into the rainforest and meet the gorillas at close quarters. The treks are carefully organized so that the gorillas and their rainforest home remain largely undisturbed. Only small groups of tourists make each trek, and they travel on foot. Experienced local guides lead them, and the tourists are taken to see only certain groups of gorillas that have grown used to human contact.

Trips to see the Highland gorillas in Virunga National Park in the Democratic Republic of Congo are carefully designed to protect these threatened animals. However, recent wars in the area have led to forest damage and gorilla killings.

21

A wildlife safari at the Masai Mara National Reserve in Africa – but who is watching whom?

On safari

People who take safari trips enjoy seeing wildlife in its natural environment. But safari trips can cause serious damage to the environment. Large numbers of minibuses travelling along the same routes erode the trails. The visitors also disrupt the feeding and behaviour patterns of the wild animals they come to watch. The waste produced by tourists can also cause damage. Animals may become ill from drinking water polluted with sewage, or from eating waste on rubbish heaps. In Kenya, for example, elephants have died from eating batteries.

Trekking holidays

The mountains of Nepal are popular for trekking holidays. In 2007 more than 400,000 people visited the area. This sparsely populated landscape is easily damaged by such large numbers of visitors. The trekkers' walking activities erode mountain trails where the soil is already thin. The building of lodges for the trekkers to stay in has damaged areas of rare rhododendron forest. Damage to the forest increases erosion further and results in greater numbers of landslides.

Leaking money

One of the main benefits of tourism, especially in poorer countries, is that it brings jobs and money to the local population. But in some cases local people do not benefit. The reason is 'economic leakage'. This is when the money that tourists spend in a place is taken by companies abroad rather than invested in the local area. It costs a lot of money to build a large tourist resort, and often local companies cannot afford to do this. Large multinational companies therefore develop the resort, and much of the money that tourists spend goes to these companies. As a result, local people can remain very poor, even though there are luxury hotels and rich tourists in their area.

PERSPECTIVE

The pros and cons of tourism

'Tourism is like a tiger with two tails. On the one hand it offers massive employment and boosts the economy. On the other hand, if not controlled, it can steal away from the inhabitants of a country most of what makes their country worth living in and worth visiting.'

Sir Laurens van der Post, South African author, philosopher and conservationist

CHAPTER 3

The Development of Eco-tourism

Most people prefer to take holidays that will benefit the local community and the environment. In the 1980s, tourism companies began to offer people more 'eco-friendly' holidays. The first of these trips were to remote areas, such as rainforests, to discover more about the wildlife. This type of sustainable tourism became known as 'eco-tourism'. The idea behind this kind of tourism is that it should bring the benefits of jobs and money to an area without damaging the environment.

Early eco-tourists were interested in visiting wild, rugged areas like this mountainous region of Patagonia, Argentina.

In the 1980s, groups of research scientists and naturalists involved in the making of wildlife film and television programmes began to study and work in areas rich in wildlife. One particular area they focused on was that of the South American rainforest. The scientists did not know this part of the world very well, so they relied on local guides and transport to get around. Later in the 1980s, the people who had been guiding the researchers and film-makers began offering trips to people such as bird-watchers, who had a strong interest in wildlife. Eco-tourism grew out of these trips.

24

SUSTAINABLE DEVELOPMENTS

Fragile islands

Islands are especially vulnerable to damage from tourism because resources such as food and water are limited. The Galapagos Islands in the Pacific Ocean have a particularly fragile eco-system. Many of the plant and animal species that live there are found nowhere else in the world. There are strict rules about tourist trips to the Galapagos. For example, most people are only allowed to visit on cruise ships and do not stay on the islands themselves. This means that tourist accommodation does not need to be built and problems of sewage and waste disposal are kept to a minimum. However, there are concerns for the future. The number of tourists is growing, and the strict tourist rules are not always enforced. Recently, for example, a company allowed visitors to fish for sharks in the Galapagos, and no action was taken against them.

A blue-footed booby on the Galapagos Islands in the Pacific Ocean. The unique wildlife of the Galapagos attracts many eco-tourists. Despite careful management, tourist numbers are damaging this precious environment.

The first sustainable holidays

The earliest eco-holidays were to rainforest areas in places such as Costa Rica and Ecuador. The tourists stayed in lodges with very basic facilities (for example, there was no running water or air conditioning). The idea was to reduce the environmental impact of the buildings by keeping the accommodation simple. Local people were employed to build the lodges, and they used local materials to do so.

The early holidays were designed for small groups, which again kept the environmental impact to a minimum. Local people acted as guides on the holidays. They described the wildlife of the area, and explained which species were under threat and the type of conservation work that was being done to protect them.

The expansion of eco-tourism

The 1990s saw a growth in people's interest in eco-tourism and in the number of commercial businesses set up to provide services for eco-tourists. In areas popular with eco-tourists, local governments also became involved. The International Eco-tourism Society (TIES) was founded to encourage eco-tourism and research ways in which holidays could be designed genuinely to benefit local people and the environment.

Various organizations, including TIES and the United Nations Environment Programme (UNEP), have drawn up a set of eco-tourism principles. The idea of the principles is to define exactly what eco-tourism involves. Three main principles are as follows:

- eco-tourism should minimize damage to the environment;
- the profits from eco-tourism should help local people or businesses and fund conservation in the area;
- as part of the holiday, eco-tourists should improve their environmental awareness by learning about the place they are visiting, the wildlife in the area, and the conservation efforts being made there.

Eco-lodges like these in Kenya, Africa, are designed to have less effect on the environment. These lodges are made from local materials. They have no running water and no electricity.

PERSPECTIVE

No sanctuary for the people?

'In the name of the Jaguar,
Please reserve some land for me.
In the name of the butterfly
Leave an acre for me . . .
In the name of the Jaguar
And in the name of the Baboon
Leave an acre of sanctuary
For Belizean man and Belizean woman
and another one for Belizean children.
We are like baboons without a sanctuary
On the edge of marginality's marginality.'

In Belize, local poet Adalbert Tucker describes the problem caused by creating national parks to preserve wildlife. He says sometimes this may involve moving local people off their land.

Numbers of tourists visiting Antarctica have grown from about 1,000 in 1987 to tens of thousands today. Antarctic scientists believe that numbers should be limited to preserve this largely untouched area.

Greenwashing

As eco-tourism has developed and grown more popular, many companies that have become involved are attracted by profits rather than environmental ideas. Many so-called eco-holidays do not follow the original principles of eco-tourism. The tours are organized by large businesses based outside the area, so most of the profits go abroad. The tourist groups are too large, and the accommodation has too much impact on the environment. The guides are not well trained, and do not explain to visitors how to avoid disturbing or even killing wildlife. These kinds of trip are simply 'greenwash' – they use the 'green' label to sell their product. Like 'whitewash', greenwash means a company does not deliver on its promise of what it claims to be.

FACE THE **FACTS**

A ten-day 'eco-tour' in Venezuela offered by one large company is pure greenwash. It involves five air flights (on top of the flights to and from Venezuela) and two nights in luxury hotels. Other accommodation during the tour consists of air-conditioned bungalows, each with a private bath, and a shared swimming pool. The trip also includes long car drives and trips in motor boats. Overall, the holiday produces far more carbon dioxide and involves more energy and water use than many 'non-green' holidays.

An eco-tourist camp in the Sahara Desert. Eco-tourists can travel by camel instead of by car. However, the flights there and back produce large carbon emissions.

Small tropical islands like this one have very fragile eco-systems that can be disturbed by quite small numbers of tourists.

Greenwashing is widespread because there are no international rules about eco-tourism. Any company can describe its holidays as eco-friendly, whether they are or not. However, some organizations do have rules about eco-tourism that can be taken as a sign of a good quality holiday. The Australian government, for example, gives an eco-certificate to holidays in Australia that have a minimal impact on the environment. There is also a sustainable tourism certificate for businesses in Latin America. Respected organizations such as TIES, UNEP and the World Tourist Organization support this certificate.

If you are thinking of going on an eco-holiday, it is important to look into how the company you are hoping to travel with carries out its business. Ask what it does to conserve the environment. What exactly does it do to improve the well-being of local people? How does it help the community? Does it offer visitors informative and educational activities to increase awareness? Find out if it has won any 'green' awards and investigate what guidebooks and other visitors say about it.

CHAPTER 4

How to Make Tourism Sustainable

Since the 1990s the number of eco-tourists has risen by between 20 and 34 per cent each year. In 1998 there were 45 million eco-tourists. It is estimated that by 2010 this number will almost have doubled. With such an increase in demand, is it possible to make sure that eco-tourism is sustainable?

Visits to national parks, such as this one in Canada, are a kind of eco-tourism because the money raised from tourism helps to protect the animals and plants living there. However, many 'safari' trips to national parks can cause damage to the environment.

The rapidly increasing numbers are one of the big problems for eco-tourism. Many of the places that eco-tourists want to visit are fragile environments. Small changes in these places can have large effects on the eco-system. It is essential that even small groups of tourists act responsibly to avoid harming their surroundings. But, as the numbers rise into the many millions, preventing environmental damage becomes increasingly difficult.

What governments can do

Governments can limit the number of tourists allowed into an area so that the tourists do not overwhelm the local population and put a lot of strain on the environment. Governments can also help to avoid environmental damage by limiting the places in which tourism is allowed to develop. In the Canadian national parks, for example, tourist development is only permitted in a few small areas. These tourist-designated sites can accommodate quite a lot of people. Other parts of the parks are open to visitors but no tourist development is allowed. The majority of the tourists enjoy a holiday where they go on short hikes close to the designated areas. Some more adventurous people go backpacking, walking along the longer trails for days or even weeks. However, only fairly small numbers of people do this, and they walk rather than drive and leave relatively little refuse behind.

Tourists take part in a guided tour of the shoreline at the Great Barrier Reef Marine Park, Australia. Experienced guides can help visitors reduce their impact on a fragile environment.

SUSTAINABLE DEVELOPMENTS

Protecting the reef

The Great Barrier Reef in Australia is the largest coral reef in the world. Parts of the reef have suffered serious damage from a combination of tourism, pollution and climate change. To protect the reef, the Australian government has set up a marine park with several zones within it. Some zones are accessible to all, others can only be used for scientific research, and others are completely off limits to all visitors. Zoning has helped some parts of the reef to recover, and has avoided the need to ban tourism and scientific research.

A local guide shows a group of university students how plants are used by people living in the Rift Valley of western Kenya. The students are staying at an eco-tourism centre called Marich Pass.

Tour companies

Tour companies that are determined to keep their holidays 'green' should avoid building too much accommodation in one area. They should use local builders, as far as possible, and choose materials (preferably local ones) that will not cause environmental damage. They should buy food locally and use local people as guides.

Tour companies can also help tourists make the most of their holiday by giving them guidelines on how they can minimize their impact on the environment. Visitors should avoid leaving litter behind or taking souvenir rocks and shells home with them; they should follow local customs and buy local products.

Pollution from transport

Many eco-holidays involve long-haul flights to reach the destination. The carbon emissions produced by air travel are the biggest source of pollution in the entire holiday. If people take holidays closer to home, they will have far less impact on the environment.

There is no way of avoiding or cutting down the carbon emissions produced by a long flight. For this reason, some people believe it is not possible to describe any holiday involving a long flight as an eco-holiday. However, tourists can 'make up' for the carbon emissions from their flight by 'offsetting' them. Carbon offsetting means paying money towards a project that will reduce carbon emissions. One such project is tree planting. Trees absorb carbon dioxide from the atmosphere during the day as part of the process of photosynthesis. Planting trees therefore reduces some of the effects of global warming. Another way of carbon offsetting is to contribute money towards the building of a solar power station or some other sustainable energy scheme.

Eco-tourists and orang-utans

The Borneo rainforest is threatened by logging and mining companies, who wish to exploit its rich natural resources. This rainforest is also the only place in the world where orang-utans are found living in their natural habitat. Eco-tourism has provided money and work to help save large areas of rainforest from mining and logging. Eco-tourists are offered a range of different tours, from short trips on which they are taken to watch and photograph orang-utans, to six-week volunteer trips where the tourists carry out conservation work in the rainforest.

CHAPTER 5

Sustainable Tourism

Eco-tourism is a fast-growing industry, but it is still only a small part (less than a tenth) of the whole tourist market. Not everyone wants to go on holiday in the wilderness to observe wildlife. But many people would like to take holidays that are sustainable. So how can we create a range of different holidays without risking damage to the environment? Making tourism in general more sustainable involves changing the way we think about how we 'go on holiday'.

Rainforest holidays were the earliest examples of eco-tourism, and they are still the most popular.

In a survey carried out by British travel agents, 45 per cent of people said they would be prepared to pay a little more for a holiday if the extra money went towards preserving the local environment. People also said they would pay a bit more if it guaranteed that the people working at their holiday destination were given a decent wage. There is evidence that tourists from countries outside the UK have similar attitudes. In recent years, some tour companies have begun to advertise holidays as sustainable, or responsible. This kind of sustainable tourism is becoming more and more popular.

A tourist walks to a yurt in the Tengeri Desert in northwest China. The bare, sandy desert in this area is slowly being transformed to green by the planting of millions of trees.

What is sustainable tourism?

Sustainable tourism means holidays that avoid the damaging effects caused by mass tourism. A sustainable holiday is one that tourists can repeat year after year, without degrading the environment or destroying the culture of the local people. Any kind of holiday can be made sustainable. It can take the form of a three-week trip to a distant tropical beach resort, or a weekend break at a campsite in the hills near home.

Conserving resources

Sustainable tourism is about conserving resources. It means using fewer materials, recycling most of our refuse and minimizing the impact of any left over waste. It means building energy-efficient buildings and using sustainable energy sources, such as hydroelectricity, wind or solar power.

PERSPECTIVE

Environmental audits

One way of making a tourist resort more sustainable is through an environmental audit. This involves studying the day-to-day operation of a hotel, ski resort or other tourist facility, and finding ways of changing how it is run in order to reduce its environmental impact. Environmental audits can help to reduce energy bills and the amount of other resources used by a tourist facility.

Sustainable tourism means making sure that local people benefit from the tourists who visit their area. Using local supplies, eating local food and employing local people are all ways of doing this. It is also important for tourist developments to fit in with the local area. The accommodation, for example, should blend in with local architectural styles or the surrounding landscape. The number of people visiting an area should be appropriate, too. So, for example, tourist numbers should be restricted in areas with limited food and water resources. Larger towns or cities, and areas with good water and food supplies, can support greater numbers of tourists.

Whitepod ski lodges are the eco-friendly way to ski. The futuristic-looking lodges are basically canvas tents, with no running water or electricity. Guests eat at a more conventional ski lodge nearby.

Good practice

For the visitors themselves, sustainable holidays need not differ greatly from other kinds of holiday. For example, a chain of hotels in Greece, run by a company called Grecotel, is similar to other hotel chains in the area. The difference is that the Grecotel hotel buildings are made using local materials, and the water supply is heated mostly or entirely by solar power. The hotel taps have flow regulators that reduce the amount of water used. Some of the waste water is collected and used to water the gardens. Much of the food served at the hotels is produced locally, and Grecotel encourages farmers in the area to grow food organically. There is careful recycling of batteries, paper, plastics and glass, and garden waste is collected to make compost.

Governments can help to encourage sustainable tourism. Lake Wanaka is a tourist resort in New Zealand. The New Zealand government has funded a sustainable tourism project in this area. Sixty-four businesses have worked with environmental assessors to develop sustainable tourism plans. As a result, the businesses have made changes, including reducing their energy and water use, recycling and composting more waste, and reducing waste by using less packaging.

Grecotel is a European business that runs a string of hotels in a sustainable fashion. Most of the food served at the hotels is grown in organic gardens like this one.

SUSTAINABLE DEVELOPMENTS

Keeping it local

Step Up Travel is a website that encourages sustainable travel in a unique way. The site carries advertisements for accommodation, businesses and activities from all around the world. This makes it possible for a traveller to arrange a holiday in a faraway country using businesses that are local to the area. The money the tourist spends goes to people in the tourist destination, not to a multinational company.

Sustainable beaches?

Although many kinds of sustainable holiday are now available, sustainable tourism has not yet made an impact on popular beach resorts and other mass tourist destinations. However, there have been some attempts to create sustainable resorts.

Between the 1950s and the 1970s, Calviá on the island of Mallorca, Spain, grew from a sleepy region to a tourist centre with accommodation for about 100,000 visitors. But there were huge environmental costs. Farming in Calviá almost disappeared, and urban areas became ten times bigger. Air pollution increased because of the number of vehicles. The biggest problem was caused by the additional demand that tourists made on the water supply. The water table (the level of underground water) fell by more than 80 per cent.

By the 1990s, tourism in the area was decreasing because Calviá was no longer the pretty beach paradise it had been in the 1950s. The local government decided to try to make tourism in Calviá more sustainable. It halted the building of tourist accommodation and ordered the demolition of many buildings along the seafronts, replacing them with parkland. The emphasis of tourism shifted from the beaches and coasts to focus on walking, golf and winter holidays. This meant that not all the tourists were concentrated on the beaches in the summer. Desalination plants were built to provide more fresh water.

The region of Calviá in Mallorca specialized in conventional beach holidays until overdevelopment forced it to change and make tourism more sustainable.

The changes in Calviá won the area a sustainable tourism award in 1997. However, there are still many problems. The region's water use has increased because the new golf courses need to be maintained. Water is now shipped in from the mainland to meet Calviá's needs. Yacht harbours have been built on areas of coast that were previously untouched. Tourist numbers are still growing, and the capacity of the local airport has recently been almost doubled to allow for this.

In New Mexico a Native American guide leads tourists around the Acoma Pueblo settlement. As at Canyon de Chelly, the guides here use their local knowledge and experience to bring alive the history and the culture of the area.

PERSPECTIVE

A sharing experience

'My grandmother said: "It's not your mouth that you learn with, but your other senses. That's why we have two of everything else: eyes, ears, nostrils, hands." Your mouth is for sharing, everything else you learn with. She never said "teach". It's sharing.'

A Navajo tour guide at Canyon de Chelly National Monument in Arizona describes the thinking behind his culture.

CHAPTER 6

A Sustainable Future?

Sustainable tourism is becoming more widespread. Successful examples from around the world show it can work, but there is a long way to go before it becomes the norm. In many places tourism is still developing in damaging ways. Although most tourists like the idea of sustainable holidays, they are more concerned about keeping the cost of their trip down and are tempted by the facilities a resort can offer. Tourist operators are business people – they are more interested in making a profit than protecting the environment. So how can we change attitudes to tourism and build a sustainable future?

Sustainable economics may offer one answer to the problem. At present, when a business looks at costs and profits, it does not take into account the environmental resources it uses. It counts these as being 'free'. But if a business pollutes the air or uses up the water supply in an area, it affects everyone, especially in a tourist resort. No one wants to go on holiday to a place that is polluted or where there is a drought.

Some experts think we need to look at the cost of things in a different way. Sustainable economics means that businesses take the environmental cost of

Cheap flights become much more expensive when the cost of the carbon emissions they produce is taken into account.

40

their activities into account. Many businesses are already looking at their 'carbon footprint' (the amount of carbon dioxide their activities release into the atmosphere). Reducing our carbon footprint is important if we are going to slow down climate change.

Sustainable costs and profits

Sustainable economics involves extending the idea of the carbon footprint to other environmental and social effects. For example, if building a tourist complex involves draining a wetland area, this counts as an extra cost because wetlands are home to a rich variety of wildlife and they help to clean up water supplies and prevent flooding. On the other hand, if a business cleans up a polluted stretch of river as part of its tourist development strategy, this action is counted as a profit.

FACE THE **FACTS**

By 2020 the number of international tourists will be likely to have risen to 1.6 billion – nearly double the number for 2006. Many more of these tourists will be from Asia (especially China and India). If destinations are going to cope with this huge increase in tourist traffic, tourism must be made more sustainable.

For these young Chinese people, the 2008 Beijing Olympics was a local occasion. By the time they are adults, many more people from China, India and other less developed countries will travel abroad for holidays or to attend sports events.

Learning more

It is important for people to find out more about sustainable tourism. When we understand what huge environmental problems face the world, then we think more carefully about the damage we do to the environment when we go on holiday. On eco-holidays, people learn about the wildlife in an area and are told about species that are threatened by human activities. This type of learning could be extended into other kinds of holiday. For example, a beach holiday could include some time on the sand dunes, learning how the plants help to bind the dunes together and how the dunes protect inland areas from flooding. This would help people understand the importance of preserving sand dunes.

In recent years the volunteer holiday has become popular. This is a form of sustainable tourism where people carry out conservation work in the places they are visiting. This can be combined with other activities to make a really fun trip. For example, volunteer holidays in Costa Rica combine surfing with work protecting sea turtles and their nests. This type of holiday is educational, and it is made a richer and more rewarding experience by the involvement with conservation work.

A student from Kansas, USA, helps to build an adobe home in Sonora, Mexico. Like many other students and young adults, she is spending her spring break on a volunteer holiday.

PERSPECTIVE

Sharing and learning

'Each traveller can take on the role of ambassador for international peace, by sharing his or her own culture and traditions and by learning those of the host country.'

John Graf, International Institute for Peace Through Tourism

Changing attitudes and actions

There are many ways in which mass tourism damages the environment. Eco-tourism offers a limited solution to the few people who have enough money and want the kind of nature holiday it offers. But eco-holidays do not reduce the environmental impact of mass tourism on popular tourist resorts. We need to develop sustainable tourism, where all holidays have a minimal impact on the environment. We also need to expose the real costs of 'cheap' flights and other kinds of mass tourism by including the environmental damage they cause in the overall holiday budget.

A great deal of research has already been done into sustainable tourism and sustainable economics. However, much more needs to be done to put sustainable tourism into practice. The most important thing to change is people's attitude. Even when we go on holiday, we need to be aware of our impact on the environment. If we do not, beach holidays on paradise islands like Maui will become a thing of the past.

Two kayakers get a spectacular view as a killer whale breaches directly in front of them. Whale-watching remains one of the most popular types of eco-holiday.

adobe A sun-dried brick used for building.

algae Plant-like organisms that live in the sea or freshwater. Most are microscopic, but seaweeds are a type of algae.

carbon dioxide A gas that consists of carbon and oxygen combined. It is the most abundant damaging greenhouse gas produced by people.

carbon footprint The amount of carbon dioxide that the activities of a person or a group of people release into the atmosphere.

climate change The gradual warming of the Earth's average climate that is resulting from pollution released into the atmosphere by humans.

combustion chamber The enclosed space in an engine where fuel is burned.

deforestation The removal of trees from an area.

desalination Turning seawater to freshwater by removing the salts from it.

developed country A country with a developed industrial base and a relatively high level of income per head of population.

developing country A country with an undeveloped or developing industrial base and a relatively low level of income per head of population.

drought A period without rain, which causes damage to food crops.

erosion The removal of rock and soil by the action of the wind, water, waves, or heat and cold.

fossil fuels Fuels made from the remains of plants and marine animals that lived millions of years ago. Coal, oil and natural gas are fossil fuels.

geologist A person whose job it is to study the origin, history, structure and composition of the Earth.

global warming An increase in the average temperature of the air at the surface of the Earth.

greenhouse gases Gases in the atmosphere that trap the sun's heat.

greenwash Giving a holiday or other product the appearance of being eco-friendly, when in fact it is not.

herbicide A chemical that is sprayed on farm crops to prevent the growth of weeds.

hydroelectricity The production of electricity by the power of running water.

microbe Any minute life form; the term is especially used to refer to harmful bacteria.

multinational A large business that operates in more than one country.

naturalist A person whose job it is to study plants and animals in their wild state.

pesticide A chemical that is sprayed on farm crops to get rid of insect pests.

photosynthesis The process by which plants, and plant-like creatures such as algae, use energy from sunlight to produce sugary food from carbon dioxide and water.

pilgrim Someone travelling, often over a considerable distance, to a holy place for religious reasons.

promontory A headland: a high ridge of land that juts out into the sea or over a lowland area.

reach (of a river) A stretch of river between two bends.

sarcophagus A stone coffin, usually from ancient Egypt, Greece or Rome.

smog A kind of unpleasant fog caused by pollution in the atmosphere.

supersonic Faster than the speed of sound (1,225 km per hour at sea level).

sustainable energy source A source of energy, such as solar power, wind power or hydroelectricity, which will continue to be available for the foreseeable future.

taberna An inn or public house in ancient Rome.

trek A long-distance walking holiday, usually in a remote area such as Nepal.

turboprop A kind of aircraft jet engine that uses propellors to push air through the engine.

water table The level below which underground rocks are saturated (soaked) with water. In dry areas the water table is deep below ground; in wet areas it is close to the surface.

BOOKS

Eco-Action: Travel of the Future, Angela Royston, Heinemann, 2007

Geography Skills: Planning for a Sustainable Future, Helen Belmont, Franklin Watts, 2007

Our Environment: Eco-tourism, Peggy Parks, Kidhaven Press, 2005

Sustainable World: Environments, Rob Bowden, Wayland, 2007

WEBSITES

www.bbc.co.uk/history/british/victorians/seaside _01.shtml
A BBC website about how the early seaside resorts became popular during Victorian times.

cooperhewitt.org/exhibitions/tourism_in_ america/site/index.asp
The Cooper-Hewitt National Design Museum website features an online exhibition about three American landscape artists – Frederic Church, Winslow Homer and Thomas Moran – who helped to develop interest in wild areas such as Yellowstone and Yosemite.

www.getty.edu/art/exhibitions/grand_tour/index. html
The story of the Grand Tour during its heyday in the eighteenth century.

www.sustainabletourism.net/cs_destination.html
This website has some examples of sustainable holidays around the world.

Page numbers in **BOLD** refer to illustrations and charts.